My Big Book of HALLOWEEN Activities

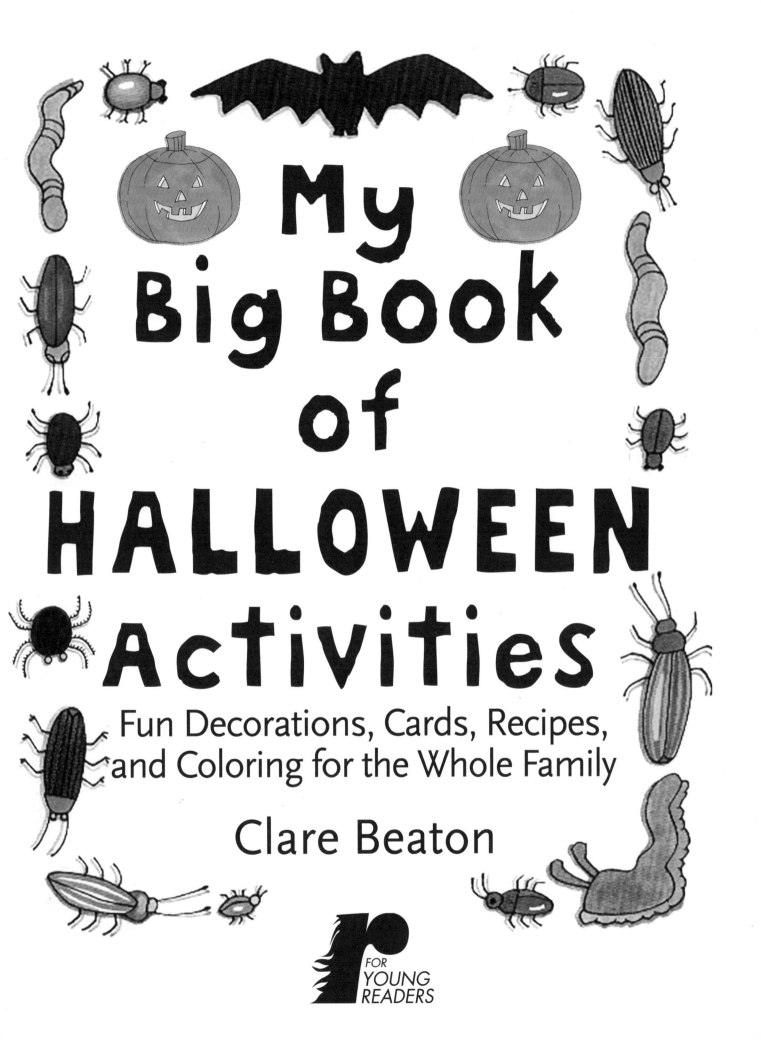

My Big Book of HALLOWEEN Activities

Fun Decorations, Cards, Recipes, and Coloring for the Whole Family

Clare Beaton

FOR
YOUNG
READERS

Racehorse for Young Readers books may be purchased in bulk at special discounts for sales promotion, corporate gifts, fund-raising, or educational purposes. Special editions can also be created to specifications. For details, contact the Special Sales Department, Racehorse for Young Readers, 307 West 36th Street, 11th Floor, New York, NY 10018 or info@skyhorsepublishing.com.

Racehorse for Young Readers ™ is a pending trademark of Skyhorse Publishing, Inc.®, a Delaware corporation.

Visit our website at www.skyhorsepublishing.com.

10 9 8 7 6 5 4 3 2 1

Library of Congress Cataloging-in-Publication Data is available on file.

Cover design by Louise Millar
Cover artwork by Clare Beaton

Print ISBN: 978-1-63158-414-5
Ebook ISBN: 978-1-63158-422-0

Printed in China

My Big Book of HALLOWEEN Activities

Treasure not Trash

Here is a selection of things you can keep to use for the projects in this book and for others too.

candy Wrappers

Keep jewel-colored foils and cellophane.

Plastic Bags

Keep thicker, colored ones. It doesn't matter if there is writing or pictures on them.

cardboard, cardboard Boxes, and Tubes

Small, large, thick, thin, and corrugated are all useful.

Large Plastic Bottles

Wash and remove any labels. See-through and colored bottles are both useful.

Old Jeans

Wash and iron old jeans even if they have holes.

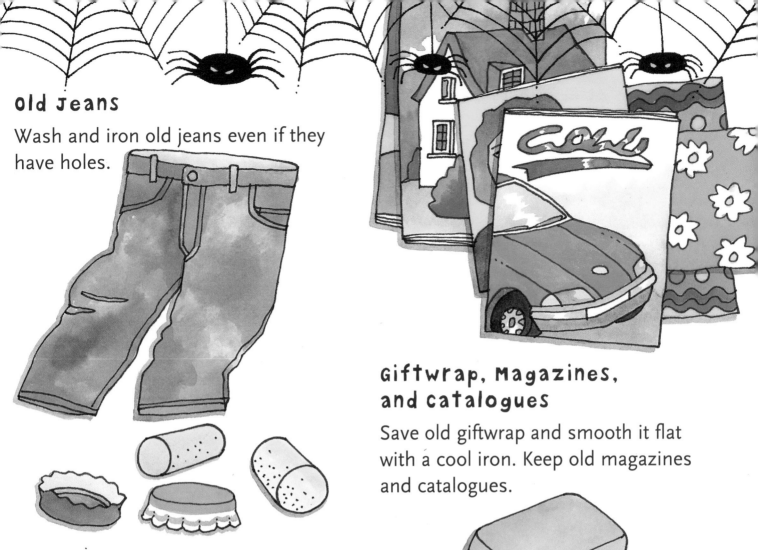

Corks and Metal Tops

Rinse bottle tops and dry them.

Buttons

Every color and size.

Giftwrap, Magazines, and Catalogues

Save old giftwrap and smooth it flat with a cool iron. Keep old magazines and catalogues.

Egg Cartons

Egg cartons are very useful. Use them for making projects or even as storage for small treasures like buttons.

Autumn Leaves

Collect them while they are dry and clean.

Before you begin

- Always take great care with sharp tools such as scissors, needles, and knives.
- Always cover work surfaces with newspaper before you start to paint or varnish your work.
- When using a craft knife always cut away from hands. Use thick cardboard or something similar under whatever you are cutting. Cut slowly and lightly several times.
- Wash your hands and wear an apron before preparing food.

Some basic tools and materials:
★ paint and brushes
★ varnish
★ glue
★ scissors and craft knife
★ paper and cardboard
★ colored pencils and felt-tip pens

This black cat will be purring through the pages with you. See if you can spot it each time.

How to trace from templates
For some of the projects you will need to trace from templates. Here's how to do it very simply and successfully.

What you will need
★ tracing paper
★ soft pencil
★ sticky tape
★ thin cardboard

1

Trace the template shape using the tracing paper and pencil.

2

Turn over the tracing paper and scribble over lines with the soft pencil.

3

Turn over and tape on to the thin cardboard. Retrace over lines.

Halloween story

Halloween is a very old festival. Hundreds of years ago the Celts who lived in Britain believed that spirits of the dead and ghosts came alive to frighten them. It was known as the Festival of the Dead.

Aaaaaaaaaaaaaaahhhh!

When Christianity arrived in Britain, a Christian festival was introduced on November 1 to replace the old Celtic one. It was called All Saints' Day or All-Hallows. But the old festival celebrated on October 31 still survived and was called All Hallows' Eve. Later the name became Hallowe'en, or Halloween.

It was a night of bonfires, games, and fun. People had their fortunes told and young people played games to see who they would marry.

An Irish legend tells of Jack—a man destined to wander over the world forever with a lantern carved from a turnip. Today pumpkins make popular lanterns.

"Trick or treat" is a traditional American form of Halloween mischief. Children knock on doors and play tricks if they don't get a treat!

Aaaaaaaaaaaaaaaahhhh!

Freaky forest

Here's how to make a dark, unfriendly forest complete with spiders, bats, and cobwebs.

Place some twigs in a large vase or jug. Pull a cotton pad carefully until it is thin and weblike. Attach it to the ends of the twigs.

Following the instructions on page 4, trace the templates on to black paper and cut them out. Glue the bats and spiders on to the twigs and "webs" or hang them on black thread.

TEMPLATES

Cotton "webs"

Halloween costumes

Costumes for Halloween can be made very easily and effectively with things that you probably already have at home.

The main color to remember when dressing up for a spooky horror party is BLACK. Wear black clothes, black headgear, and black accessories. Add some chains and a blue or purple streak in your hair and you will give everyone the creeps!

Spooky jewelery

Makeup
White faces

Black eyes and mouth

Black or purple
   nail polish

chains
Hang silver chains on your jeans and wear them around your waist.

clothes
Black pants, T-shirts, skirts, and tights. Black fishnet tights can be worn on your arms too!

witch's cat

What you will need
★ close-fitting black clothes
★ stiff black paper
★ hairband
★ black material for tail
★ black thread and needle
★ black face paint
★ sticky tape
★ scissors

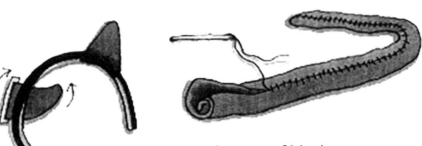

Cut two triangles out of black paper and stick to hairband. Roll black material into a sausage and sew along edge. Sew or pin onto cat's bottom. Using black face paint, draw yourself whiskers and a black nose.

skeleton

What you will need
★ close-fitting black clothes
★ white sticky-backed plastic
★ white cardboard or large white paper plate
★ black felt-tip pen
★ thin elastic
★ scissors

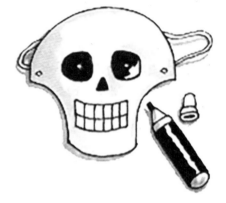

Look at the bone shapes on page 27. Draw your own (to fit the person) on the sticky-backed plastic and cut them out. Don't worry if they look a bit wobbly! Stick in position on the black clothes—this is best done when the clothes are on. Cut the paper plate or card into a skull shape and draw on the face with black pen. Make a small hole in each eye socket. Then attach the thin elastic to fit.

Ghost

What you will need
★ old white sheet
★ black felt-tip pen
★ black paper
★ glue
★ scissors

Drape sheet over head. Carefully mark where the eyes are with the pen. Remove the sheet and cut two small eyeholes. Make a length of white or silver paper chain and hold or drape around neck. If necessary, fasten the sheet with safety pins on to clothed shoulders!

Shine a flashlight from under the sheet for an extra-special look.

Glue here

Be careful to round off corners with scissors.

Dracula

What you will need
★ black jacket or waistcoat
★ black trousers
★ white shirt
★ black cardboard
★ thin elastic
★ white plastic cup or yogurt container
★ scissors
★ white and red face paint
★ hair gel

Cut a bow tie shape out of black cardboard and attach thin elastic. Cut teeth out of white plastic cup or yogurt cup. Get dressed— paint face white with red "blood" dribbles from corners of mouth. Put teeth into mouth and gel back hair.

accordion pumpkins

What you will need

★ orange paper
★ scissors
★ pencil and tracing paper
★ black felt-tip pen

Draw on faces in black felt-tip.

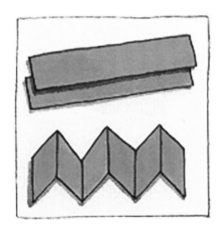

Cut the paper into 21 in. x 3 in. strips. Fold each strip like an accordion.

Trace the pumpkin template from page 23 on to the top of the paper.

Hold together and cut out, taking care to leave the paper joined on each side. Open out.

For how to trace templates see page 8.

window pumpkin

What you will need
★ orange paper
★ pencil and scissors
★ yellow tissue paper
★ sticky tape

Cut a pumpkin shape out of orange paper. Draw and cut out eyes, nose, and mouth.

Cut two squares of the tissue paper big enough to cover the holes for the face.

Tape the tissue paper on to one side. Stick up in your window.

"Trick or treat" bag

When you go out "trick or treating" you will need a bag to collect all your goodies.

What you will need
★ black plastic sack
★ scissors
★ plastic shopping bag
★ sticky tape

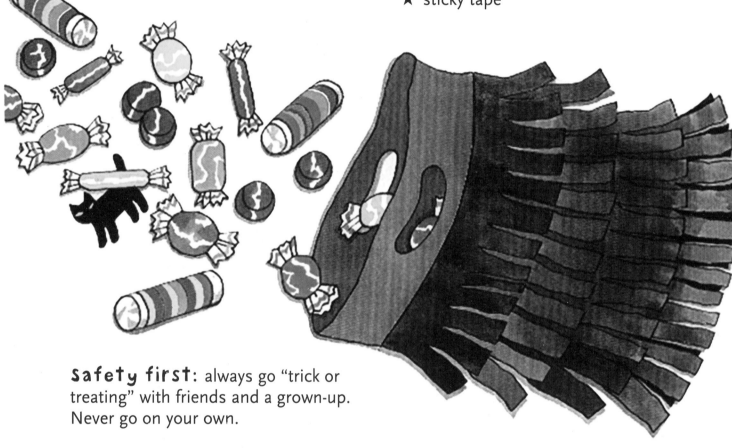

safety first: always go "trick or treating" with friends and a grown-up. Never go on your own.

1

Cut the black plastic sack into 5 in. wide strips. Cut strips into fringes.

2

Start from bottom of bag.

With sticky tape across the top, stick fringes around the shopping bag.

3

Cut off extra fringe at the edge.

Overlap each layer. Finish off just below handle.

Scary spider!

Why not make lots of these spiders and hang them all over your room and really scare your friends and family!

What you will need
★ black paper
★ tracing paper and pencil
★ scissors
★ sticky tape
★ thin black elastic or yarn and needle
★ yellow sticky paper or paint

SPIDER TEMPLATE

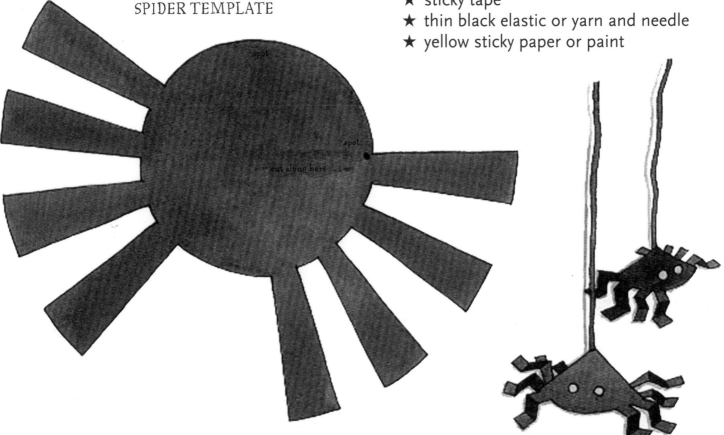

spot
spot
cut along here

Don't forget to mark the spots on your spider.

Bend legs three times as shown.

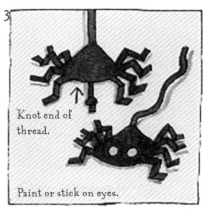

Knot end of thread.

Paint or stick on eyes.

Follow the instructions on page 4 to trace the spider template above on to black paper. Cut it out.

Cut where shown and form a cone matching the spots. Fix with tape.

Using the needle, pull a length of yarn through the center of cone. Hang up.

Broomsticks & slime

See who can climb the broomsticks and avoid slipping down the slime to reach the top first.
You will need to make counters like those on page 26, a die, and two or more players.
Play the game like Chutes and Ladders. Take turns to throw the die and move along the squares.

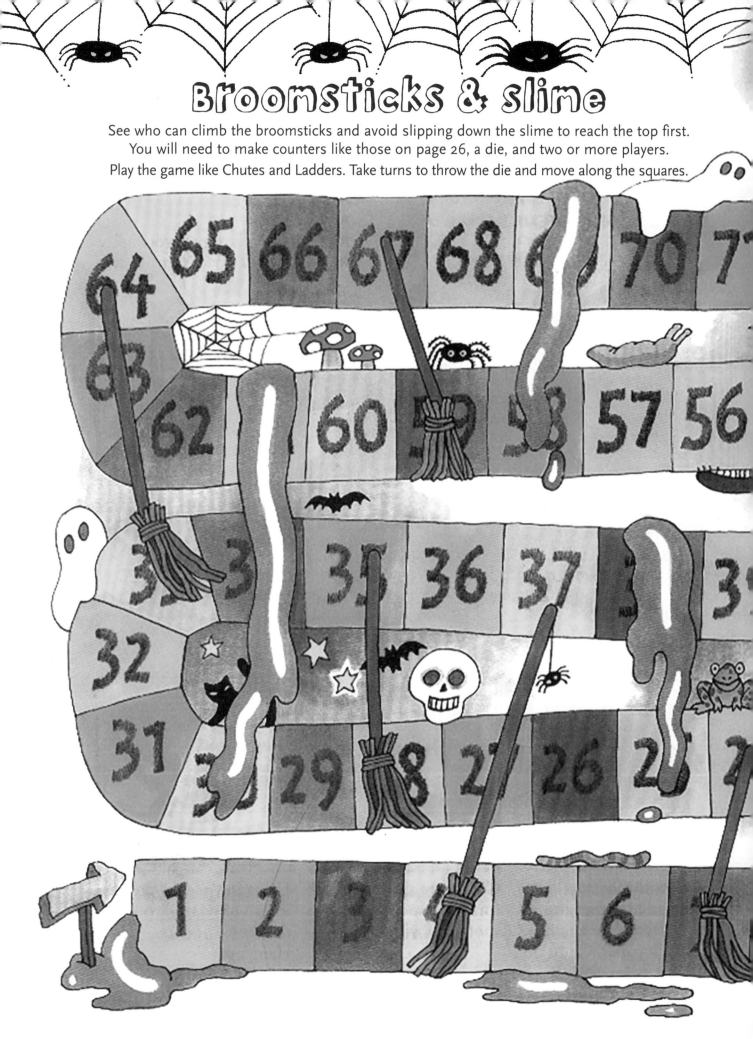

spider webs

You can make lots of these in different creepy colors! Why not make some of the spiders on page 13 to go with them?

What you will need

★ tissue paper
★ scissors
★ sticky tape

1 Fold a square of tissue paper into four. Fold once again into a triangle.

2 Cut the end opposite the point into a curve.

3 Carefully tear strips out of the paper from the one folded edge, stopping before you reach the other edge.

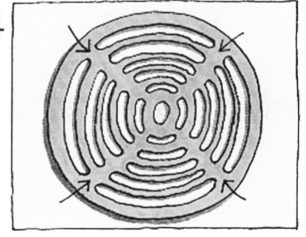

4 Open the web out and stick up with tape at points shown.

Fiendish faces!

Simply wear black clothes to show off these dramatic faces.

warning—be careful not to paint too close to your eyes. Tie hair back and avoid getting face paint on clothes. Always follow printed instructions and ask a grown-up before applying hair colors.

What you will need
★ face paints
★ sponges and brushes
★ hair colors and gels

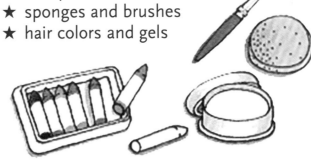

Slime

Using a sponge, color face yellow. Draw or paint edge of slime in green. Fill in rest with a sponge.

Scarface

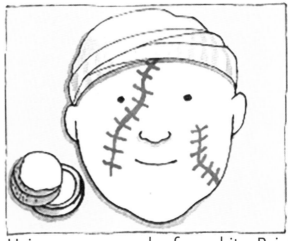

Using a sponge, color face white. Paint on scars with a small brush and red face paint. Hide hair under a hat.

Mummy

Using a sponge, color face white. Paint black bandage lines across face with brush.

creepy crawly

Color hair green and gel it if you like.

Using a sponge, color face orange. Paint on insects, worms, and spiders with a small brush and black paint.

Halloween masks

Use the template on page 26 to make these exciting masks!

Spider web

Make a white cardboard mask. Draw on a black web and hang small plastic flies and spiders from black thread.

Vampire

Cut the mask out of purple cardboard extending the top into points. Paint black eyebrows. Dot with glue and sprinkle on glitter. Wear with vampire teeth!
(See page 9)

Night owl

Cut a fringe from a black plastic sack and stick around an orange mask. Paint on patterns in white and black. Trace beak template on to orange paper, cut out, and glue on along flaps.

Beak

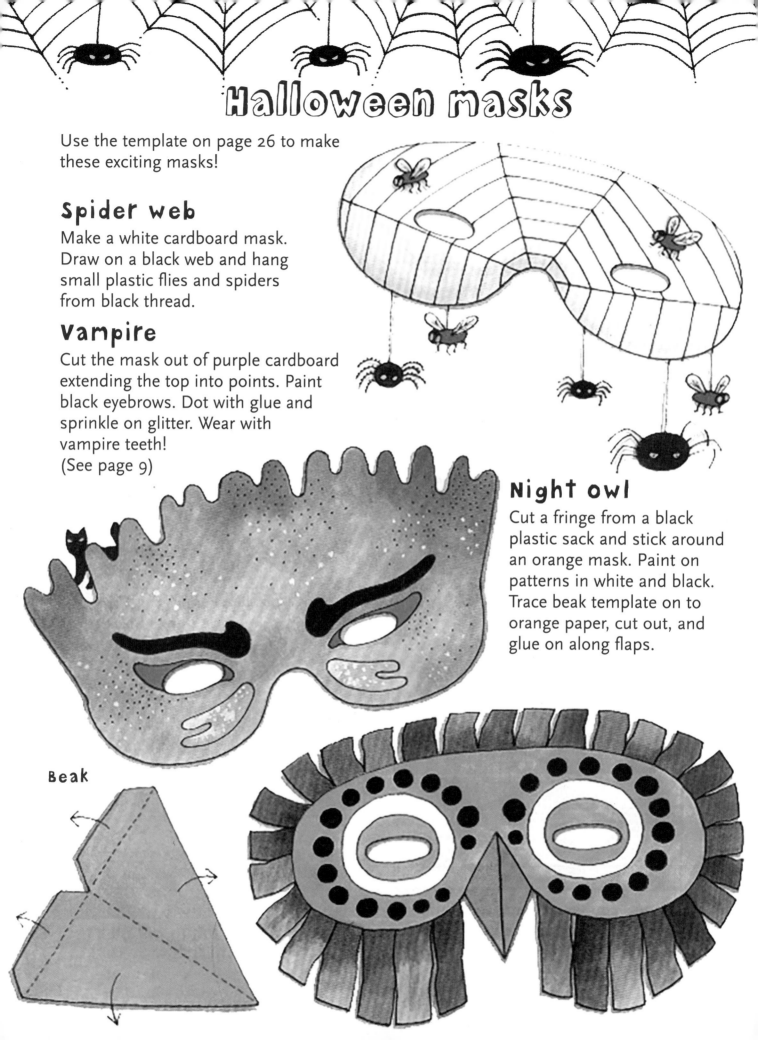

Toffee apples

What you will need
★ 10 apples, washed and dried
★ 10 wooden sticks

For the toffee
★ 1 3/4 cups soft brown sugar
★ 3 tbsp + 1 tsp butter
★ 1/4 cup + 1 tbsp corn syrup
★ 1 tsp lemon juice
★ 3/4 cup water
• heavy-based saucepan
• wooden spoon
• bowl of cold water
• oiled greaseproof paper

Ask a grown-up to help you make these as the toffee gets very hot.

Remove stalks and push sticks firmly into apples.

1 Put the toffee ingredients into the saucepan and heat gently until dissolved. Stir occasionally.

2 Increase the heat and boil rapidly until a dollop of toffee becomes hard when dropped into cold water.

Make sure they are completely covered in toffee.

3 Remove from heat. Carefully dip each apple in the toffee. Then plunge it into a bowl of cold water.

4 Stand the apples on oiled greaseproof paper until the toffee has set hard.

Spot the difference

Can you spot ten differences between these two pictures?

Eyeball cakes

What you will need

- ★ 1/4 cup + 3 tbsp softened butter
- ★ 1/2 cup sugar
- ★ 1/2 cup + 2 tbsp self-raising flour
- ★ 2 eggs
- ★ 1/2 cup + 3 tbsp powdered sugar
- ★ small packet of chocolate buttons
- ★ red food coloring

- bowl
- wooden and metal spoons
- 18 paper cake liners
- cupcake tin
- small brush

1

Cream the butter and sugar together until pale in color and fluffy.

2

Beat in the eggs one at a time with a tablespoon of flour with each. Fold in rest of flour with metal spoon.

3

Cool on wire rack.

Spoon equal amounts into 18 paper liners standing in cupcake tin. Bake in the oven at 375°F for 20 minutes until risen and golden.

4

Mix sugar with 1 tablespoon of hot water until smooth.

When cool, cover top of cakes with icing. Place a chocolate button in center. With the small brush, draw veins on icing in red food coloring.

creepy mobile

Make a scary Halloween mobile using the templates on the opposite page.

What you will need

★ thin cardboard or stiff paper
★ pencil and tracing paper
★ scissors
★ paint and brushes
★ colored foil or sticky shapes
★ needle and black thread
★ twigs tied in a bunch

1

See page 4 for how to trace templates.

Trace the templates onto the cardboard or stiff paper and cut out. Make several of each shape.

2

Decorate with foil, paint, and shapes—don't forget to do both sides.

3

Cut pieces of thread to different lengths.

Make a small hole at the top of each shape with the needle and thread. Pull thread through, knot, and hang from twigs.

Halloween craft tips

Have a look at pages 2 and 3 to see all the kinds of things you can keep to recycle. Old clothes, plastic bags, and cardboard boxes are not trash at all! The symbol ⟳ in the list of things for each project shows you where you can use them. There are also more template shapes specifically for the activites on these following pages and simple instructions on how to use them on page 50.

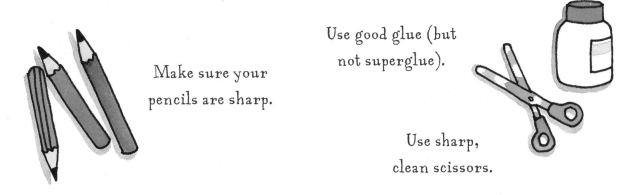

Make sure your pencils are sharp.

Use good glue (but not superglue).

Use sharp, clean scissors.

Before you start on a project make sure you read it through and get everything you need ready. Work on a clean, flat surface with plenty of room. If you need to use scissors, knives, the iron, or the oven, be careful and have an adult standing by.

Dressing up

cloak

- ○ black plastic trash bag
- ○ sticky tape
- ○ needle and thread
- ○ scissors and ruler
- ○ holographic tape (optional)

Cut a 2.5-in. wide strip off the top of the trash bag. Cut the bag open along one side and the bottom.

Sew a line of running stitch along the long, straight edge.

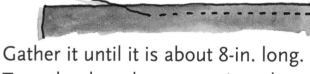

Gather it until it is about 8-in. long. Tape the thread to secure it and remove the needle.

Tape the strip along the top. Keep the ends free for tying together.

Open up the trash bag and cut one long edge into points.

Decorate with the holographic tape if you like.

Mad Hair

Transform yourself with some crazy-colored hair.

- ○ plastic bags ♻
- ○ scissors
- ○ sticky tape
- ○ old hat or Witch's or Wizard's hat from page 32

Cut the handles off the bags.

Tape the uncut edge inside a hat. Add more layers to make a fuller wig.

Cut in from the cut edge to make a fringe. Make the strands either 0.5 or 0.75 in. wide. Stop 1.5 in from the top of the bag.

Leave a gap for the face at the front of the hat. Add a shorter fringe at the front if you like.

Witch's or Wizard's Hat

- large pieces of stiff, black paper
- pencil and ruler
- scissors
- sticky tape
- pair of compasses

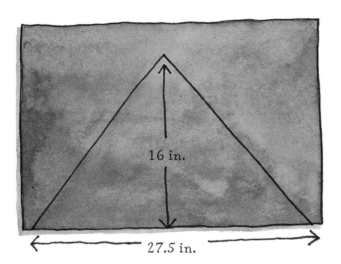

Draw a large triangle onto the paper and cut it out.

16 in.

27.5 in.

Place the cone onto more black paper and draw around it.

Draw another circle 1 in. inside the first one. Then draw another circle 3 in. outside the first circle. Cut out around the largest and the smallest circle.

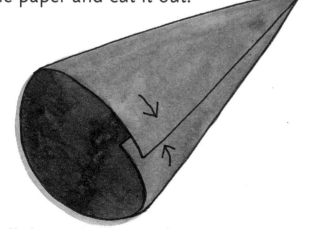

Pull the paper around into a cone to fit your head. Tape along the side. Trim the bottom until it is even.

Cut between the hole and the middle circle to make a fringe.

Decorations

Use the star and moon templates on page 50 and some colored or gold and silver paper to decorate your hat.

Fold the fringe up.

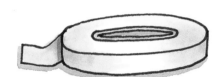

Use tinsel or holographic tape too.

Push the fringe into the bottom of the cone and tape it inside.

33

Trick or Treat

skeleton mask

- old cereal box
- black paint or thick black felt-tip
- thin elastic
- tracing paper and pencil
- scissors

Use the instructions on page 50 to trace the template on to the inside of the box. Cut it out. Fill in around the eyes and jaw with black paint or felt-tip. Draw on teeth and a nose. Measure the elastic to fit around your head. Thread it through either side of the mask where marked. Knot the ends.

SKELETON MASK
TEMPLATE

Bat Mask

○ stiff, black paper
○ 2 sequins
○ tracing paper and pencil
○ thin elastic
○ scissors

Use the instructions on page 50 to trace and cut out the mask. Glue the sequins on for eyes. Measure the elastic to fit around your head. Thread it through either side of the mask where marked. Knot the ends.

BAT MASK
TEMPLATE

Trick or Treat Bag

This bag can be decorated for Halloween and then used afterwards without the special decorations.

- ○ pair of old, washed jeans
- ○ 59 in. thick cord or rope
- ○ needle and thread
- ○ pins
- ○ scissors
- ○ safety pins (optional)

Depending on the size of the jeans and the size of bag you want, either use the whole of the top of the jeans or just half.

Cut off the legs and pin the cut edges together along the bottom. Sew together. If using half, sew up the side as well.

Thread the cord through all the belt loops and knot the ends together. Draw tight to close the bag. Put it over your shoulder to check the length. If too long, undo the knot, cut one end, and retie.

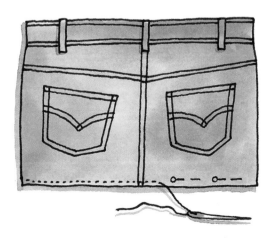

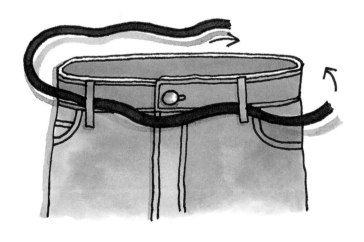

Decorations

Use the templates on page 50 to draw and cut out some Halloween shapes. Use colored paper.

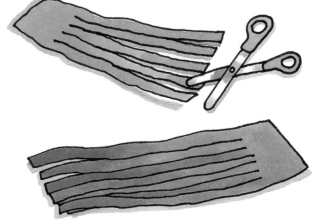

Holographic tape can be stuck on to the bag to make it glitter in the dark.

Stick them on both sides of the bag.

Make some plastic bag tassels. Cut green, orange, or black bags into fringes. Attach to the bag with tape or safety pins.

Halloween Decorations

Pumpkin Lantern

This is THE traditional Halloween lantern. Use the pumpkin flesh to make the soup on page 42.

- ⭕ pumpkin
- ⭕ sharp knife
- ⭕ metal spoon
- ⭕ felt-tip pen
- ⭕ tea light

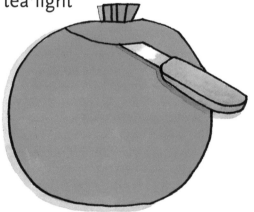

Ask an adult to help you cut the top off the pumpkin.

Draw a face on one side of the pumpkin with the felt-tip pen.

Scoop out the flesh with the metal spoon leaving a shell about 1 in. thick.

Cut out the eyes, nose, and mouth with some adult help. Place the tea light inside. Light it, replace the lid, and put the lantern in a safe, level place.

Rustling Ghost

You can hang one or more of these outside so that they blow and rustle in the wind.

- ⭕ white trash bag
- ⭕ sticky tape
- ⭕ dry, fallen leaves ♻
- ⭕ string and scissors
- ⭕ black felt-tip pen

Draw out your ghost shape on the trash bag. Draw some eyes.

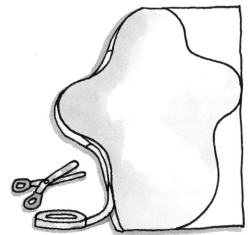

Cut out and tape the sides together as you go. Leave a large hole at the top.

Stuff leaves into the hole until the ghost is full, taking care that the sides do not split. Tape up the hole.

Tape a length of string to the top and hang up in trees or bushes.

Ice House Lantern

A very unusual and pretty lantern that is great fun to make!

- ◯ 1 packet of white sugar cubes
- ◯ 1 packet of powdered sugar
- ◯ water
- ◯ bowl
- ◯ round-ended knife and wooden spoon
- ◯ tea light
- ◯ metal plate or tray
- ◯ silver cake decorations (optional)

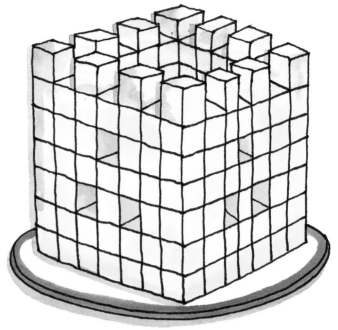

Mix some powdered sugar in the bowl with cold water to make a thick paste. This is the "cement" for the sugar cube "bricks." Make more of this mixture as you need it.

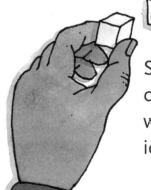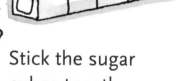

Stick the sugar cubes together with the sugar icing on the sides.

Start building your lantern on the plate or tray. Make a base measuring seven cubes square.

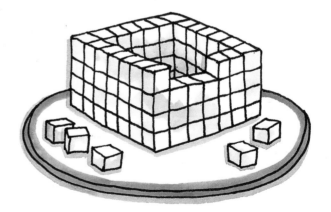

Keep adding more sugar cubes on top, spreading a little icing on the sides, tops, and bottoms.

Continue building up the four walls. Keep them even and, before you run out of cubes, work out how many you need to finish.

Place the tea light inside, light it, and place the lantern in a safe, level place.

Decorate with silver balls stuck on with powdered sugar paste.

variations

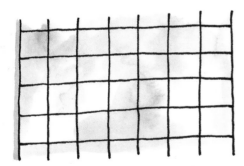

Leave out some cubes for "windows."

Build more lanterns with different patterns at the top.

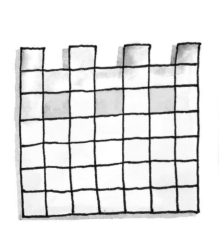

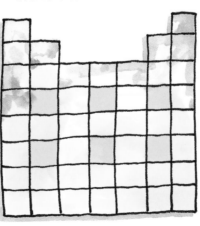

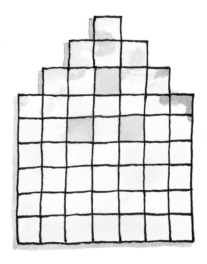

Festive Food

Pumpkin Soup

Use the flesh from the Pumpkin Lantern on page 38 to make this delicious soup. Ask an adult to help with the cutting and heating.

- 8 cups pumpkin flesh (no seeds or fibrous bits)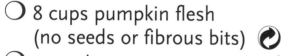
- enough water to cover pumpkin
- chicken stock cube
- 2 1/2 cups milk
- salt and pepper
- cinnamon or nutmeg

Drain the liquid and throw it away. Whiz the pumpkin in a blender or food processor until smooth.

Cut the pumpkin into chunks. Put it all in the saucepan and cover with cold water. Crumble the stock cube into the pan.

Bring to the boil and simmer until the pumpkin is tender.

Pour the pumpkin back into the saucepan. Add the milk, pepper, and salt. Stir over a low heat.

Serve with a shake of cinnamon or nutmeg on top.

Ghost Toast

- ◯ loaf of sliced bread
- ◯ butter or margarine
- ◯ shredded coconut
- ◯ raisins
- ◯ chocolate chips
- ◯ round-ended knife

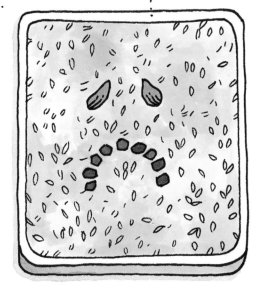

Put on the raisins and/or chocolate chips to make a mouth and eyes.

Spread the butter or margarine over the slice of bread.

Ask an adult to help you put the bread under a hot grill until the chocolate has melted and the coconut has turned golden.

Sprinkle thickly with coconut.

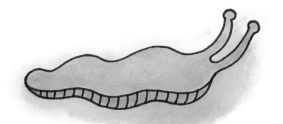

Crunchy Nutmeg Muffins

The carrot and banana make these muffins moist inside and this contrasts nicely with the crunchy topping.

Makes 10 or 15 small muffins

- ○ 1 small ripe banana
- ○ 1 large carrot weighing about 5 oz.
- ○ 3/4 cup + 3 tbsp sunflower oil
- ○ 3/4 cup light muscovado sugar
- ○ 3 large eggs
- ○ 1 1/4 cup self-raising flour
- ○ 1 level teaspoon freshly grated nutmeg

Preheat the oven to 375°F.

Beat the oil, sugar, eggs, mashed banana, and grated carrot together in a bowl.

Peel and mash the banana. Peel and coarsely grate the carrot.

Then sift the flour into the bowl. Fold it into the mixture with the nutmeg.

Carefully spoon the mixture into paper cases in a muffin tin. Fill to the top.

Use two teaspoons to make this easier.

Topping

- ⚪ 2 tbsp light muscovado sugar
- ⚪ 1/2 level teaspoon freshly grated nutmeg
- ⚪ 1/2 cup oat flakes

Mix all the ingredients together and sprinkle over the muffins.

Bake them on the middle shelf of the oven for 25 minutes until well risen and cooked through.

Cool on a wire rack and keep in an air-tight container.

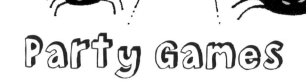

Party Games

Apple Bobbing

A traditional game popular at Halloween and great for parties.

- ○ apples
- ○ large bowl
- ○ water
- ○ towel

Fill the bowl with cold water. Place on a table and put in the apples.

Guests have to take turns to try and pick up an apple with their mouth with their hands behind their backs.

Wipe faces with the towel!

Hat Hoopla

Use the Witch's or Wizard's Hat on page 32 for this game.

- ⭕ Witch's or Wizard's Hat
- ⭕ thick cardboard (from a cardboard box) ♻
- ⭕ paints and brush

Make some rings from the card, following the measurements below.

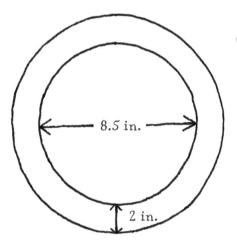

8.5 in.

2 in.

Make about six and paint them in Halloween colors. Leave them to dry.

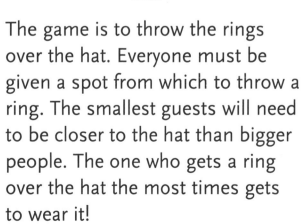

The game is to throw the rings over the hat. Everyone must be given a spot from which to throw a ring. The smallest guests will need to be closer to the hat than bigger people. The one who gets a ring over the hat the most times gets to wear it!

ghostly storytelling

This is a fun thing to do at the end of a party or "Trick or Treating." Turn the lights down and get everyone to sit comfortably.

You need a storyteller with a good ghost story and some listeners.

Each listener is given one or two pieces of paper with a word on it together with the noise it makes. For example, "wind (whistling)." When the word is spoken by the storyteller the listener immediately makes that noise.

It's important to remain quiet, otherwise everyone will miss their word. Some listeners might have more than one word to listen out for.

At first the words aren't mentioned too often but, as the story goes on, they become more common. At the end the words are mentioned all at once and this will give a very noisy finale!

There is a story opposite to give you the idea. You can add more words and noises to go along with your own story.

OWL (hooting)

TOM (Go away!)

WOLVES (howling)

WIND (whistling)

MICE (squeaking)

TOAD (croaking)

WITCH (cackling)

GHOST (wailing)

FOOTSTEPS (thump thump)

CAT (meowing)

CLAWS (scratching)

MAKE AND color
Spooky
Things

How to to make these spooky things

From page 63, there are ready-drawn cards, masks, and decorations for you to color. Cut along the solid lines and fold along the dotted lines.

For coloring in, you can use colored pencils, crayons, felt-tip pens, or paints. Start coloring the center of the cut-outs first. Leave borders for last so you don't smudge them.

Use fairly thick paint and wash your brush between colors. Leave the cut-outs flat to dry. Don't forget to add your signature on the back of the cards!

On page 63 there is a template which can be used to make envelopes for some of the cards. Then you can send them to your family and friends.

Keep the rest of the book. It has lots of other ideas on how to make more spooky things. There are also templates and stencils to help you.

Some things you will need:

★ plain and colored paper or thin cardboard

★ tracing paper

★ pencil and ruler

★ scissors and craft knife

★ glue

★ sticky tape

★ black trash bags

★ gold and silver paints

★ crayons, paints, and felt-tip pens

★ thread and thin elastic

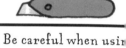

Be careful when usir a craft knife.

54

Spooky doorway

Decorate a doorway with black plastic garbage bags cut into strips. For really long streamers, cut the sides of the bags and double the length of the strips.

Don't cut right to the top.

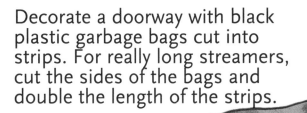

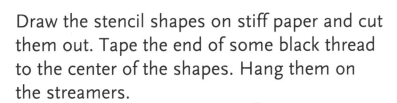

Draw the stencil shapes on stiff paper and cut them out. Tape the end of some black thread to the center of the shapes. Hang them on the streamers.

Tape along the top of a door—and make a surprise entry!

Envelopes

Make some colorful envelopes for
your cards using the template
on page 63.

What you will need:
★ colored paper
★ pencil
★ tracing paper
★ ruler
★ scissors
★ glue

1 Follow the instructions on
page 55 to trace the template
onto paper, using a ruler to
help. Cut it out.

2 Fold along the dotted lines.
Glue the bottom flap on to the
two side flaps. Put the card in
and glue down the top flap.

Use the stencils
to decorate the
envelopes.

Emma

Joe Brown
17 High Road
New York, NY 12345

Templates

Follow the instructions on page 55
to use the templates on the following pages

Template

Party name cards

Color in. Write the name on the bottom half of the cards. Use a craft knife to cut out the shape *above* the dotted lines. Fold along the dotted lines.

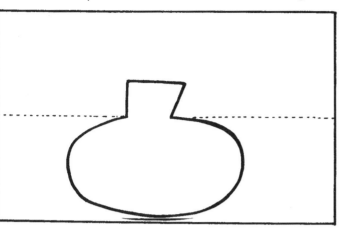

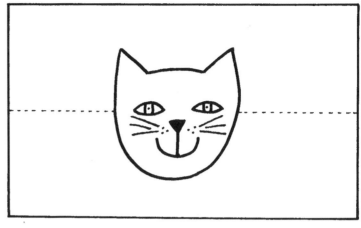

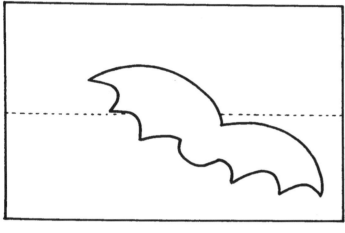

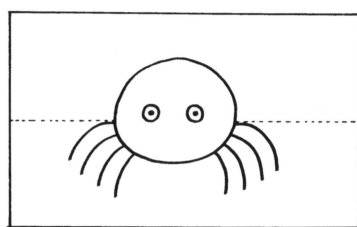

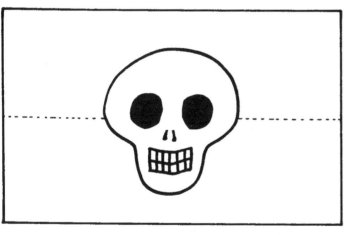

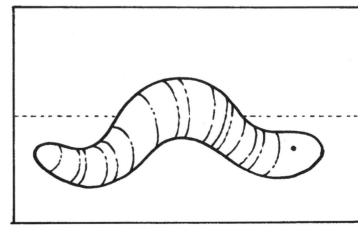

kull face mask

olor in black around the eye holes, nostrils, and jaw.
ut out the mask. Be careful with the eye holes.

_hen thread elastic through the holes. Strengthen the holes with sticky tape on the back.

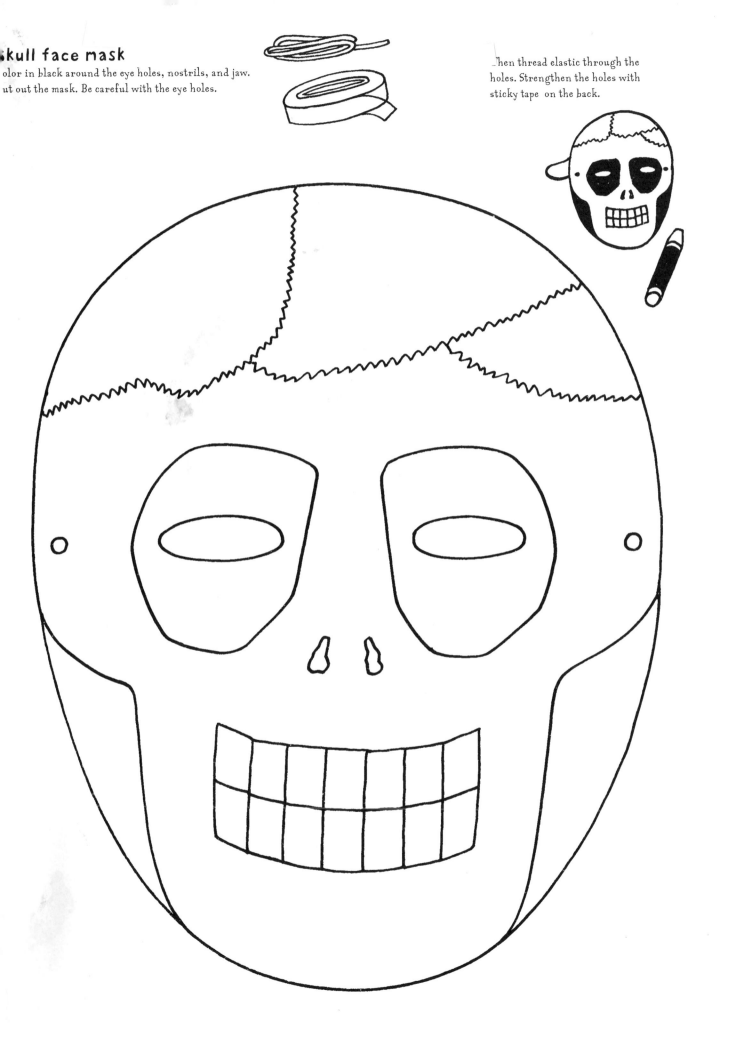

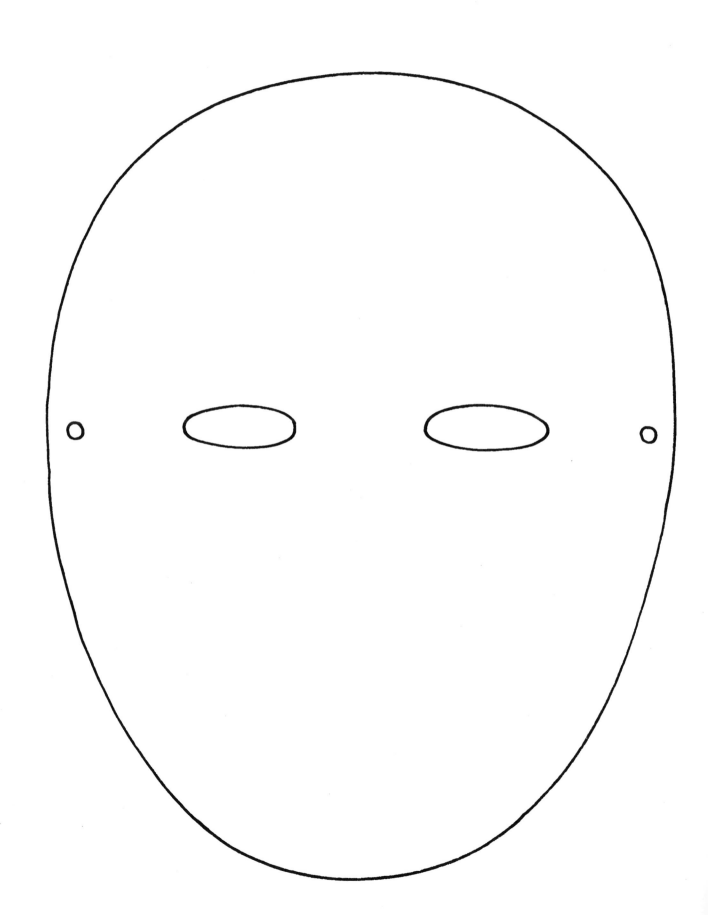